Presentations that Work

Practical Tips on How to Make GREAT PowerPoint Presentations

Norman S. Wei

2012 Edition

This publication is designed to provide accurate and authoritative information about the subject matter covered. It is sold with the understanding that the publisher is not engaged in rendering legal, accounting, or other professional services. If legal advice or other expert assistance is required, the services of a competent professional person should be sought.

© 2012 Norman Wei
All rights reserved.

This publication may not be reproduced, stored in a retrieval system, or transmitted in whole or in part, in any form or by any means, electronic, mechanical, photocopying, recording, or otherwise, without the written permission of Environmental Management and Training, LLC., P. O. Box 152239, Cape Coral, Florida 33915

Table of Contents

Preface 4

Chapter 1: Special Tips on Making Great PowerPoint Presentations 5

PowerPoint as a Visual Tool 7

Open with Five Slides 10

Chapter 2: The Three Main Points of Presentation 13

The Vioxx Story (non-bullet points in action) 15

Why PowerPoint Makes Us Stupid? 20

Chapter 3: 20 Key points about PowerPoint Presentation. 23

Chapter 4: Handling nervousness during the presentation 41

About the Author 45

Preface

This is a book on presentations. How to get your points across to the audience without having them fall asleep.

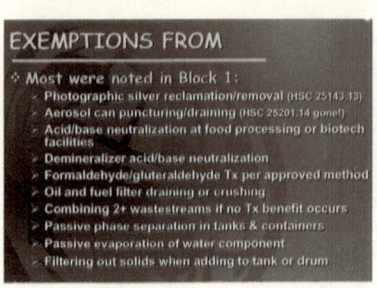

Many people do not know how to make presentations. They are very good at preparing PowerPoint slides with all the bells and whistles.

Most of the slides are jammed with 10 or more dreadful bullet points in fonts so small that no one in the back of the room can read.

And many presenters will simply read off each bullet point - one by one - until the entire audience lapses into a coma.

This book gives you practical tips on how to prepare your PowerPoint presentations and deliver them without boring your audience to death.

Chapter 1: Special Tips on Making Great PowerPoint Presentations

PowerPoint by Microsoft has become the de facto tool that most consultants use for making presentations. Unfortunately, many consultants fail to use PowerPoint in an effective manner. The most common error consultants do is to load up their slides with bullet points and/or text that the audience can barely read from afar.

Do not confuse your PowerPoint presentation with your written proposal. They are not the same. Your proposal should contain all the details of what you plan to do for your clients written out in complete sentences and paragraphs. Your proposal should describe your firm's capability, your understanding of the client's problems and your proposed approach to solving those problems.

The biggest mistake many consultants make is to try to use PowerPoint to present their entire proposal by cramming 10 bullet points on each slide to summarize all the technical details. The result is a distillation of some important information that will inevitably be lost in the hierarchical structures of the bullet points.

A classic example of the misuse of PowerPoint can be seen as a result of the following tragic incident.

When the Columbia space shuttle broke up in re-entry to the Earth's atmosphere in 2003, the President appointed the Columbia Accident Investigation Board (CAIB) to look into the causes. As part of the, the Board looked into how those engineers and contractors at the National Aeronautical and Space Agency (NASA) transmit their technical information to their management. The Board observed that "generally, the higher information is transmitted in the hierarchy, the more it gets 'rolled up,' abbreviated, and simplified. Sometimes information gets lost altogether, signals drop from memos, problem identification systems, and formal presentations. The same conclusions, repeated over time, can result in problems eventually being deemed non-problems".

The Board also found that one avenue by which information gets "rolled up" and confused, was through the technology of PowerPoint presentations.

When NASA discovered that a piece of foam had fallen off the shuttle during take off and had impacted its wing, a team of engineers and scientists began a series of analyses to assess any risk that such impact would have upon re-entry. The concern was that the damage done to the wing during take off might impair its ability to withstand the tremendous heat that would be generated when the shuttle began its re-entry into the Earth's atmosphere. That turned out to be the fatal cause of the incident.

On Day Nine of the mission, the engineering team presented the results of its risk assessment findings to NASA management in a PowerPoint presentation while the shuttle was still in space. One of the critical slides used in the presentation contained six levels of hierarchy.

According to the Board, important engineering information was either "filtered out or lost in the small prints within the bullet points."

The CAIB concluded: "When engineering analyses and risk assessments are condensed to fit on a standard form or overhead slide, information is inevitably lost. In the process, the priority assigned to information can be easily misrepresented by its placement on a chart and the language that is used. . . . As information gets passed up an organization hierarchy, from people who do analyses to mid-level managers to high-level managers, key explanations and supporting information is filtered out. In this context, it is easy to understand how a senior manager might read this PowerPoint slide and not realize that it addresses a life-threatening situation. . . . The Board views the endemic use of PowerPoint briefing slides instead of technical reports as an illustration of the problematic methods of technical communication at NASA."

PowerPoint as a Visual Tool

One of the key points to remember is that presentation is more about inspiration than information. You are trying to inspire your future clients to hire you. Details of your proposal are already in that half inch thick three-ring binder on the desk in front of your client.

When you open up your word processing program, the screen is usually in portrait format – just like a book or your technical proposal. On the other hand, the PowerPoint screen is always in landscape format. In other words, the width of the screen is always larger than the height. It is just like your TV screen or the movie you watch in a theater.

Why is that?

Because PowerPoint is a visual communication tool. It is **not** a written communication tool like your proposal.

That is precisely the reason why you should never cramp your PowerPoint presentation slides with words. Visuals work a lot better in landscape format. That's why movies do not have words written all over the screens. Subtitles are all they have.

The most effective way to do a presentation is to tell a story by framing the setting, identifying the protagonist, describing the action, and offering an ending.

Just like a Hollywood movie. You are telling a story.

The key point to remember is that much of the presentation will be done by the presenter's narration. The headlines and graphics in each slide provide only the visual impact and backdrop for your story telling. Your story is not a novel because you do not need to spend many words describing the setting. The visuals in your slides do that for you. Your presentation is really more like a movie script supported by PowerPoint's graphics and visual effects.

For the audience, it is like watching a movie or documentary with you as the narrator – going from scene to scene.

In your slide presentation, each slide should contain only one complete sentence (that's the headline) and it should be supported by simple graphics or photographs that reinforce the message contained in that single headline. The headline should be written in conversational tone. Research in multi-media presentation has shown that given this format, your audience will quickly scan the headline and sit back and pay attention to what you have to say. This is a much more effective way for you to communicate your ideas to the audience than to have them dart around ten bullet points or trying to read a massive amount of text on the screen.

Dr. Richard Mayer, a well-known authority on multi-media research and Professor of Psychology at the University of California in Santa Barbara, has done extensive research in the field of multi-media presentations. His findings can be summed up as follows:

> 1. *Multimedia Principle:* Students learn better from words and pictures than from words alone.
> 2. *Spatial Contiguity Principle:* Students learn better when corresponding words and pictures are presented near rather than far from each other on the page or screen.
> 3. *Temporal Contiguity Principle:* Students learn better when corresponding words and pictures are presented simultaneously rather than successively.
> 4. *Coherence Principle:* Students learn better when extraneous words, pictures, and sounds are excluded rather than included.
> 5. *Modality Principle:* Students learn better from animation and narration than from animation and on-screen text.
> 6. *Redundancy Principle:* Students learn better from animation and narration than from animation, narration, and on-screen text.
> 7. *Individual Differences Principle:* Design effects are stronger for low-knowledge learners than for high-knowledge learners and for high-spatial learners rather than for low-spatial learners.

First of all, forget about all those psychology terms like "Modality Principle", "Coherent Principle", etc. They are just jargon used in the trade to make laymen feel stupid. Every profession has its own set of jargon.

The first finding shows that people learn better (absorb more) from a presentation with both pictures and words rather than just a bunch of words.

The third finding shows that people learn better when the words and picture appear at the same time. That means none of this fading and fading out, zooming in and zooming out, flying in from the side stuff. The more animation you add to your slides, the more DISTRACTED your audience is going to be. If you must show animation, show them a short movie.

The fourth finding tells you to stick to the basics and not to throw a bunch of words (bullet points) on the screen. Narration (you talking to the audience) is a much more effective way to communicate.

Open with Five Slides

The first five slides in a presentation are the most important. They define the story and set out the rest of the presentation. Cliff Atkinson suggests you tell your story this way:

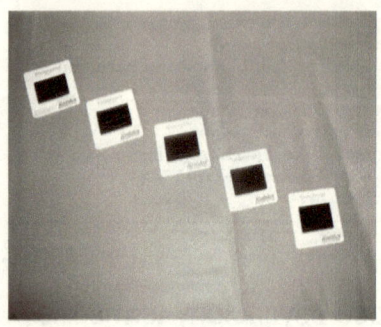

1. Define the setting (the topic of your story)
2. Identify the protagonist (main player in your story)
3. Describe the imbalance (the place where the protagonist finds himself)
4. Describe the balance (the place where he wants to be)
5. Offer a solution (how he can get there)

Imbalance is what exists, the balance is what is desired, and the solution is specifically how you propose to bridge the gap between what exists and what is desired. In other words, the imbalance is the problem that your future clients are facing. The balance is what they wish to happen. Your job as a consultant is to show your future clients how you propose to bridge that gap.

Presentation of an idea is really an art. It consists of three components:

<u>Contents</u>. These are the ideas in your proposal.
<u>Composition</u>. This is the right amount of details in your presentation.
<u>Performance</u>. This is how you deliver your presentation.

Each of these three components is a necessary but not sufficient condition for success in conveying your idea to your clients. All three must be present and done well for you to succeed. A good outcome will only happen when all three components are done well.

A presentation with good contents and composition but poor performance will yield a bad outcome. Your clients will either not understand your great ideas at all or if they do they will say to themselves: "Well, the ideas seem fine but we don't much care for the presenter."

A presentation where all three components are bad will of course result in rejection.

A presentation with bad contents and composition but excellent performance will likely get this response: "Well – we don't care much for the ideas but he seems likes a nice fellow." Another rejection will be sure to follow.

In other words, your performance at the presentation can be no better than the material you are presenting. But good material or ideas can be easily ruined by bad performance. And this happens often.

Chapter 2: The Three Main Points of Presentation

You can use as many slides as you need in your presentation. But make sure you only present only ONE point per slide. The bad habit of jamming 12 bullet points in a single slide really started some 30 years ago when people had to pay someone to make 35mm slides for their projector. And the cost was $3 or $4 per slide. So people jammed as much information as possible into a single slide in order to save money.

Remember: You can now make as many PowerPoint slides as you need. They are all FREE!

If the job you are seeking is highly technical in nature, the details of the content should be in your written technical proposal.

Using the principles described above, here are 5 simple slides prepared for a proposal to perform environmental audits for a multi-national corporation.

The 5 slides frame the story by describing the setting, identifying the protagonist, outlining the imbalance and balance and offering a solution.

Slides	What your slides are doing
Environmental laws allow citizens to sue companies for violations	This slide provides the setting for the story: Congress has enacted environmental laws that allow private citizens to take companies to court if the agencies fail to take enforcement action against the violators. It answers the question "where are we?" for the audience.
Large companies with violations and deep pockets are most vulnerable	This slide identifies your clients as the protagonist in the story. It answers the question "who are we in this setting?" for the audience. It tells your clients that if they have on-going violations of their permits, they could become targeted.
They can be sued for millions of dollars by environmental groups	This slide shows the imbalance in the story. Those environmental groups could come in and sue your clients and disrupt their business. Your clients are exposed to this imbalance because they have deep pockets and also they have on-going violations.
Regular environmental audits can prevent violations and citizen lawsuits	This slide offers your clients a way to be rid of the imbalance and return to normalcy. You then start the process of bridging that gap.

Slides	What your slides are doing
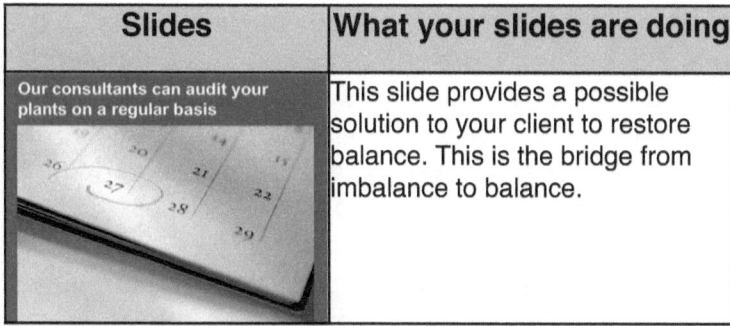 Our consultants can audit your plants on a regular basis	This slide provides a possible solution to your client to restore balance. This is the bridge from imbalance to balance.

After these initial 5 slides, you then go on to tell your clients that you have arrived at a solution to solve their problems. This is where you go through the details of your auditing plans with your audience. You can add as many slides as you need but each slide should have only ONE complete sentence describing a main point of your program. So if you have twenty main points, add twenty slides.

The Vioxx Story (non-bullet points in action)

The following is a very interesting story as reported in the Los Angeles Times on April 19, 2006. It illustrates how powerful a good presentation can be:

A Houston trial attorney who was suing Merck & Co. on behalf of a client who died while taking the painkiller Vioxx hired Cliff Atkinson (the expert who developed this new no-bullet point approach to PowerPoint presentations) as a consultant to help with his opening statement in the case. They generated a 253-slide presentation that was so mold-breaking and riveting for the jury that it was dubbed "CSI: PowerPoint" by the media. They used the 253-slide presentation as a very powerful storyboard to tell a story in the place of just presenting a long list of bullet points.

The slides provided very powerful visual impacts on the jurors. For example, instead of saying that the defendant's marketing strategy overpowers obstacles, the attorney showed a picture of a steamroller and then said it. This combination of verbal and visual effects helped drive the message home.

The attorney started by referring to the drug company's executives as "Desperate Executives" - after the TV show "Desperate Housewives". He then used simple slides (one point per slide with appropriate graphics) to illustrate that the company was desperate to rush an unsafe new drug Vioxx to the market because its existing pipeline of drugs was running dry. He told a compelling story to the jurors.

In contrast, the defense attorney "read much of his presentation and illustrated it only with hard to read excerpts from documents whose meaning was shrouded in medical jargon."

According to the newspaper, reporters covering the trial singled out the slides, with one reporter calling them "frighteningly powerful." The trial jurors apparently agreed: They awarded the plaintiff's family $253 million – which worked out to be $1 million per slide!

The jurors not only paid attention, they remembered the presentation!

Here is another example of how to use the first 5 slides to open a presentation:

Slides	What the slide is saying
A big client is looking to hire a new consultant	This is the setting of the story.
It is now your turn to make your sales presentation	This slide identify the protagonist - the person who will be making the presentation.
Your audience may fall asleep during your presentation	This is the problem faced by the protagonist. This is the "problem state"

Slides	What the slide is saying
You want your presentation to stand out from the crowd	This is the solution to the problem. The place where the presenter wants to be.

This is the "solution state". |
| Stop using those Bullet Points will get you there | This slide shows how you can go from the problem state to the solution state. If you stop using those dreadful bullet points, your audience will not fall asleep. |

Here is another example on how to start your presentation with the first 5 slides.

Let's say you are a bridge contractor and you are trying to convince the government to build a new bridge to ease congestion:

Slides	What the slide is saying
The Tacoma Narrows Bridge is the only bridge to the Olympia Peninsular	This is the setting of the story. There is only one bridge between the main land and the Olympia Peninsular in the State of Washington.

18

Slides	What the slide is saying
The Washington State DOT (WSDOT) is responsible for the traffic flow — Washington State Department of Transportation	This slide identifies the protagonist - the agency that is responsible for managing traffic flow on the bridge.
Traffic over the bridge was very congested	This is the problem faced by the protagonist. The bridge traffic is terrible. This is the "problem state".
WSDOT would like to reduce the congestion	This is the solution to the problem. The place where the protagonist wants to be. This is the "solution state".
Adding a new bridge will ease the congestion	This slide shows how you can go from the problem state to the solution state. If the protagonist were to another bridge along side the existing bridge, it would greatly ease the congestion.

After you have presented the first 5 slides, you then go on to use as many slides as you need to present your case to the WDOT that you are the right contractor for the job.

Why PowerPoint Makes Us Stupid?

"PowerPoint makes us stupid". That is a direct quote from Gen. James N. Mattis of the Marine Corps, the Joint Forces commander at a military conference in North Carolina. He of course spoke without PowerPoint. "It's dangerous because it can create the illusion of understanding and the illusion of control," General McMaster said in a telephone interview afterward. "Some problems in the world are not bulletizable."

This 4-star general is well known for his brusque and outspoken comments. But he also subscribes to Aristotle's famous dictum on effective communications: Know your audience. He talks like a marine when he is addressing a group of marines. When he is speaking to diplomats, he uses diplomatic language.

Brig. Gen. H. R. McMaster, who banned PowerPoint presentations when he was a Colonel serving in Iraq likened PowerPoint to an internal threat. He was adamant that those dreadful bullet points not be used in briefings by his staff.

Below is the infamous Pentagon PowerPoint slide that prompted a general to say: "If we can understand that slide, we will have won the war."

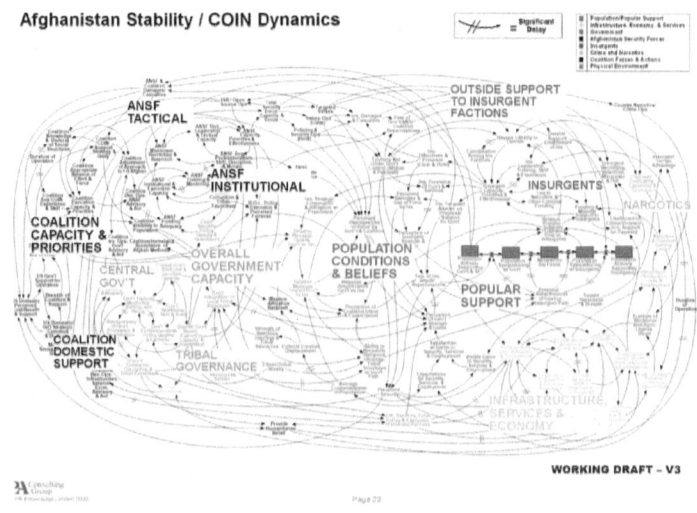

There is a similarly pervasive problem in the business world.

Company executives started replacing written reports with PowerPoint presentations (loaded with bullet points) about 20 years ago. The executive would present slides packed with bullet points at a business meeting. He would proceed to speak at length on each bullet points. That was fine albeit half the audience would be in a semi comatose state by the end of the meeting.

The REAL problem came when the PowerPoint slides were passed on down to the lower level staff for implementation. There were no backup documentations. No detailed analysis. Nada. Since none of these lower level people attended the executive meeting and never heard the presentation, they had no idea as to the nuances embedded in the presentation. All they had was a bunch of notes in bullet points and that's where everything started to go wrong: misunderstanding, misinterpretation, miscommunication, hallucination….etc.

Millions of dollars of mistakes have been made because of this problem.

If you make your sales presentation to your future clients in these bullet points, you run into the same danger of the clients not having detailed documentation of your proposal and approach.

Always back up your oral presentation with a written proposal.

Chapter 3: 20 Key points about PowerPoint Presentation

Henry Boettinger is a communication expert who was a senior executive at AT&T. In his book titled "Moving Mountains", he says "presentation of ideas is conversation carried on at high voltage -- at once more dangerous and more powerful." This book is by far the best book on how to persuade people to your point of view. All the principles discussed in this book is still valid even though it was written back in 1969.

Your PowerPoint presentation is a direct reflection of your ability as a speaker to converse with your audience. They are going to judge your team's performance based on how well they like the presentation – your story.

Remember that your presentation must include all three key elements: contents, composition and performance.

Here are a few pointers to keep in mind:

1. <u>Show passion in your presentation</u>. It was the German philosopher George Hegel who said: "Nothing great has been accomplished without passion." It is very important for you to show passion when you are presenting your slides. Your future clients need to know that you truly believe in what you are saying and that you have the desire to do the work if they award it to you. They need to know that you have not made the same old boring presentation to 100 other customers and they are now victim number 101. They need to get the sense that your presentation is the most important presentation you have ever made in your career. Your passion must show

through. In other words, the best presentations are the ones that carry high voltage. When you present your reasons for your ideas with passion, the combination will work magic.

In his book "Moving Mountains – the Art of Letting Others See Things Your Way", Henry Boettinger states that "passion and reason can cut through the fabric of doubt, inertia and fear" that your audience may have about your idea.

Passion and reason are like the blades of a pair of scissors. They go together. Neither one can cut the fabric alone.

2. Focus your clients' attention on you. Do not load the slides down with words that are mostly unreadable from afar. Even if they are readable, you should refrain from using them because the text on the screen can be a great distraction to your audience. You want them to listen to what you and your team have to say rather than try to decipher what's on the screen. The best way to get attention is to give it. You want your clients' attention on you. So when you do your homework and demonstrate that you truly understand your clients' problems, you will get attention from your clients.

Another way of keeping your audience's attention is to vary your tone of voice throughout the presentation. Never use a monotone. At various stages of your talk, your tone could go from slow to fast, loud to soft, humorous to serious and melancholic to joyful. Use plenty of interesting and out-of-the-ordinary examples. If you are describing an aerodynamic equation, explain to the audience how it describes the flight of a bumble bee. Examples like that would certain keep your audience's attention on you. Tell stories from your experience that captivate your audience. A presentation does not and should not be dull.

The difference between a presentation with variety and one without is like the difference between a river and a canal. If you are floating down a river, it offers you different surprises at every bend. You may go from farmland to gorges to forest just by floating along. A canal, on the other hand, is a man-made ditch that is straight and not very interesting. A good presentation is a river. A bad one is a canal.

3. <u>Your presentation is not about your ego.</u> It is about your ideas. So avoid reciting your and your team members' qualifications ad nausea. The fact that you are now before your future clients making a presentation means that they already know about you. Or they know you well enough to offer you their valuable time to listen to your ideas. The only time you want to emphasize your team's qualifications is when they have specific relevance to your solution.

4. <u>Don't try to be too clever</u>. There is a quote from Napoleon that pretty much sums up the danger of being too clever. We see that often in bad PowerPoint presentations. The presenter clutters up his slides with all those animations and cheesy clip arts on top of the 10 bullet points. All these special effects do nothing but make the audience dizzy. They distract the audience from the message.

The audience sit there wondering how the next batch of bullet points are going to appear. Are they going to fly in from the left? Or from the right? Or are they just going to dissolve first and then explode? Which bells are going to ring and which whistle will be blown? It is all utter nonsense.

Napoleon once said this: "*The art of war does not require complicated maneuvers; the simplest are the best and common sense is fundamental. From which one might wonder how it is generals make blunders; <u>it is because they try to be clever.</u>*"

Listen to Napoleon! Keep it simple and don't try to be clever.

5. <u>Make sure your presentation is concise and to the point</u>. Sometimes less is better. You want to focus your presentation on the key points and not on some peripheral information. If you focus, you will show your audience that you have taken the extra time and effort to distill complex issues into an understandable format. It gives them a level of comfort in deciding to hire you because they trust you will exert even more effort to solving their problems once you are being paid.

    Do not fall into the trap of wanting to tell them everything about you and your firm and hoping something will stick with the audience. It usually doesn't work that way. All that does is confuse your audience. You will end up with comments like: "What is he getting at?" It is better to repeat a few good points in your presentation than to cover a lot of good and bad points once.

    Many consultants assume incorrectly that their clients equate quantity with quality. They think their clients will feel they are getting their money's worth if the consultants submit a voluminous report. Nothing is further from the truth. There is a very good reason why corporate executives demand one-page memos from their staff. So brevity is the key here.

You certainly don't want your client to describe your presentation as "a tale told by an idiot; full of sound and fury, signifying nothing."

It is not necessary for you to cover all possible combinations and permutations in your proposed solution to the client. Just present enough to make your point. Most speakers pick three main points they want to convey to the audience and stick to them. Why? They have know they have a better chance of convincing the audience of the three points than spraying the audience with 20 points.

Information overload does not work in presentations.

If you are in a cooking contest, do you cook a couple of your best dishes for the judges to decide? Or do you prepare your entire repertoire of 30 dishes and expect the judges to try them all?

Poor speakers try to cover everything under the sun in a one-hour speech because they are fearful that someone will scream out: "Hey, you leave out one thing". What you want to do is to employ a technique known as "cognizant omission" used by many professional speakers. For example: You start by telling your audience that you have looked at all possible scenarios and you have narrowed them down to three that are worthy of further discussions. In that way, no one in the audience is going to think that you have ignored or overlooked some salient points of your argument.

And once you feel that you have convinced your audience to your way of thinking, stop pressing the point.

In other words, quit while you are ahead and stop drilling when you strike oil.

Extremely brevity is of course just as bad as excessive verbosity. It forces your audience to guess at what you are trying to say. If you can strike the proper balance between this and verbosity, you will have achieved elegance – a term easier to recognize than to describe. In mathematics, an elegant solution is one that is arrived at with the least number of steps in the least convoluted manner.

6. <u>Remember that a presentation is a "conversation"</u>. You are talking to your future clients about what you plan to do for them. It should not be a monologue. In any conversation, there should be at least two people involved. So try to engage your clients early during your presentation. Get them to talk to you too or at least acknowledge your presence!

The best way to do that is to invite your audience right up front at the beginning of your presentation to interrupt you any time they have any questions – up to a point. You don't want to be spending 10 minutes of your valuable time answering a peripheral question from one member of the audience. But you do want to engage the audience. It is a delicate balance you need to maintain. When your future clients start asking questions, it  is a clear sign that they are paying attention to you and they have engaged you and you'd better have some pretty good answers. That's probably why Henry Boettinger used the word "dangerous" in his definition of presentations. This brings us to the next point.

7. <u>Always prepare your team for any anticipated questions</u>. As you go through the rehearsal, ask yourself what kind of questions will your future clients be asking about your presentation? Make sure you have answers to all these questions. If you are going to suggest any new or not-so-well-known technology as part of your proposal, you should know that someone in the audience will have doubts about it. That doubt may linger in his mind throughout the entire presentation and he may not even ask your any question about it. But the doubt will be there. What you need to do is to address any anticipated doubt, concerns or fears that your audience may have before anyone raises them.

For example, you can say: "We understand this is a relatively new technology. However our research has shown that it will work in your situation. Here are some specific case studies of how your competitors have used this technology to great success." The bottom line is that you do not want any doubts to fester in your audience's minds.

Very often, someone in the audience may fear that your new idea or concept may make his own idea look bad. If that is going to be the case and you sense that fear, you should address it right away and reassure the individual that your new idea is really quite compatible with his. Ease his fear head on so that he can re-refocus his attention on your presentation.

When was the last time you had a conversation with a friend or business associate when you got to talk non-stop for 50 minutes before your friend could chime in? You must learn to "listen" while presenting and the best way to do that is to have the audience ask questions DURING your presentation. This is the best way to develop rapport and dialog with your audience. In reality, very few people in the audience will actually ask questions during your 50-minute talk. But the fact that you offer that opportunity to the audience makes them feel at ease, valued, wanted and appreciated.

Also learn to "listen" with your eyes. When you see someone in the audience who has this puzzled look on his face, you know you have lost connection with him and you need to reconnect with him and the rest of the crowd. You do that by asking the audience "Does this make any sense to you?" This will give you a chance to elaborate on your idea and get your point across. If you see someone passed out in a deep coma, you will know your 10 bullet points per slide has done its trick!

8. <u>Be sure to make contact with your audience</u>. The best way to get your message across to your future clients is to establish some sort of rapport or connection. If there is an opportunity for you to meet the audience before your presentation, take full advantage of it. Talk to them. Get as many names as possible and remember them. During the presentation, you can establish connection with your audience by making eye contacts with them. You want them to feel that you are having a private conversation with them.

In the Vioxx trial, it was reported in the press that the plaintiff's attorney "went through 80 slides, rarely breaking eye contact with the jury." Each slide had a picture on it with two or three words. He was able to communicate his thinking verbally to the jury as if he was having a private conversation with each juror. It was also reported that the defense attorney, on the other hand, read most of his opening statement directly from his PowerPoint slides and hardly ever looked up at the jury. There was no connection with the jury.

9. <u>Pay attention to your posture during your presentation</u>. If at all possible, do not spend all your time standing or hiding behind a lectern with both hands firmly grabbing the sides. Stand in front of it or lean against it with your elbow. Walk around it once in awhile if you can. The point here is to have as much free space between you and the audience. This reinforces the idea of intimacy with your audience. You are having a direct conversation with them.

   Remember those Presidential debates? The candidate who does well at these debates is usually the one who takes the trouble to walk out in front of the lectern or into the audience when answering a question posed by a voter. By doing so, the candidate is seen as making connection with the voter.

10. <u>State the problems clearly and early</u>. The first task you ought to do at the presentation is to clearly state the problem. If your audience does not see a clearly defined problem, it becomes restless, bored and resentful to your ideas. You identify for your audience a clear description of the problems that you are planning to solve for them. Do not fall into the trap in which many enthusiastic inventors find themselves when presenting their inventions to venture capitalists. These inventors are so excited about their inventions that they jump right in and describe how their new discoveries work. After ten minutes or so of listening to such display of energy, the audience say to themselves or worse yet out loud: "So what?" These inventors fail to tell the audience up front what problems their inventions are designed to solve. They fail to clearly state the problem.

The same bad outcome can befall a consultant if he  starts his presentation by telling his future clients how great his company is and how many offices he has in so many countries. The response is also going to be: "So what?" unless that information is really relevant to the problems at hand.

In the 5-slide example shown in this chapter, the stated problem is your clients' potential liability to citizen lawsuits. You state it early on in the presentation and then proceed to offer a solution to minimize your client's liability.

11. <u>Be forceful in your presentation</u>. No client wants to hire a mousy or timid consultant. Whatever you do, don't let them see you sweat. And don't let them sense your fear or nervousness. You may be the world's expert on the topic at hand, if your audience sees you sweat, some of them will think that's because you are not sure of your subject. This judgment is probably unfair to you. But perception is reality. Your audience will always expect you to have more knowledge on your presentation topic than they do. After all, that's why they have invited you to give them a talk on your ideas. When they sense that you are nervous and seemingly unsure of yourself, they will tune you out and reject your ideas altogether.

Remember that people seldom buy an idea without first buying the originator of that idea. They will judge your ideas by the way you present them.

12. <u>Make sure you maintain continuity</u>. If you have multiple presenters at your meeting with your future clients, you

want to make sure that the individual presentations are tied in together and they are coherent. The best way to do that is to insist that each presenter makes specific reference to either the one presentation before or after him. There is nothing more irritating to an audience than to listen to five seemingly disjointed presentations from the same team.

In general, you should try to keep your team as small as possible. The project leader should be the one to make the bulk of the presentation. If there are specialized area where a particular expertise is required, have the expert in your team speak to it briefly. Do not have a "dog and pony" show and have a cast of ten trooping through the presentation. Some consultants try to use the "dog and pony" approach to show their clients just how well they work as a team. Unless the transitions between the speakers are seamless, your future client is going to think you are doing a school play where every kid gets a talking role and the parents and grandparents get their photo shots.

Make sure your team leader introduces the speakers' topics and ties them together at the end of the presentation. The leader should also be the one to direct questions from the audience to the individual speakers. It is also the responsibility of the leader to make sure that the questions from the audience are answered satisfactorily. You are demonstrating to your future clients how your team will work for them once they hire you.

13. <u>Always start with an opening statement that holds your audience's interest</u>. There are four subject categories that will guarantee to perk up an audience. These are: royalty, religion, sex and mystery. As a consultant in the technical arena, your choices are pretty much restricted to mystery.

Using the 5-slide presentation example shown earlier, here is a possible opening statement that will hold the attention of the audience:

"Thank you for the opportunity to speak with you. I would like you all to picture this scene. We are at the reception after a very successful shareholders' meeting of a multinational corporation. The CEO is very pleased that his preferred slate of directors for his Board has been approved by a majority of the shareholders. He and his guests are enjoying the fine food catered by a world famous chef. Just as he is getting ready to go up to the podium to give a speech to thank the shareholders who have supported his slate, a well-dressed man walks up to him and hands him a document. It is a letter from an environmental group giving the CEO 60-day notice that it intends to file a citizen lawsuit against his company for failing to meet his waste water discharge limits in his permit. We are here to present to you a proven way that your company can inoculate against such lawsuits."

This statement sets the stage and offers an element of mystery leading the audience to wonder what that proven inoculation might be.

14. <u>Never read text off your slides and never apologize</u>. There are two things you should never do. You should never read your text out loud word-for-word. And you should never apologize for any short comings that you may think you have in your presentation. It is impossible for many people – except professional actors – to read a text to an audience and make it sound conversational. Once you start doing that and all your audience can see is a bald head, you lose eye contact with your audience and they get bored.

You should not apologize because if your apology sounds like false modesty, you audience will notice it and will resent it. If your apology is sincere, the audience will soon find out about your incompetence. Very often, your public speaking style is not as bad as you think because many people are a lot more critical on themselves. So why apologize in advance if your audience won't even notice it.

Many people use bullet points in PowerPoint slides as their teleprompter. The bullet points act as speaking notes to remind them of the topics. That's fine except they forget that people who make speeches with teleprompter NEVER share their speaking notes with their audience. And that's exactly what you are doing when you flash those bullet points on the screen for everyone to see and read.

There was this business development manager for a large consulting firm who made a presentation at a hazardous waste training seminar. He stood up before the audience and started to apologize for the fact that he was neither an engineer nor scientist and had little grasp of the technical knowledge in his presentation. He then proceeded to read out loud word-for-word 30 pages of text on hazardous wastes that someone had apparently handed him in the morning. And he left the podium. Before he finished, several members of the audience stood up and asked: "Why did we pay $1000 to listen to you read out loud on something you know nothing about?"

15. <u>Try to speak your audience's language</u>. Do not use technical jargons especially if your clients are not engineers or scientists who are familiar with your jargons. You cannot expect your audience to understand and accept your ideas if you speak a language they do not

understand. It shows disrespect for your clients and nothing good will come out of it. Even a non-English speaking foreigner who is charged with murder will get a translator to tell him what is happening in court. Why shouldn't your audience get the same rights?

You should also avoid using a lot of acronyms. Experts in their own fields are notorious for doing that. They assume their audience is familiar with those acronyms and pepper their talks with them. An instructor at a seminar on the Clean Air Act did that one time and the entire class was in a near coma after he had used his 15th acronym.

Successful military officers (many 4-star generals) are well known for having the ability to speak their audience's language. When they are addressing their troops in the battlefield, they use language that the enlisted men can understand. When they go before a Congressional hearing or when they are negotiating deals with foreign diplomats, they use a completely different language.

"Speaking your audience language" goes beyond the spoken words. Your attire should be appropriate for the audience. When you are speaking to a group of engineers at a tropical retreat where the dress code is informal, do not show up wearing a three-piece suit. It will just make you look silly and completely out of place. If you are not sure about the dress code at a presentation forum, come dressed in jacket and tie. You always have the option of taking them off to match the audience's attire.

They call it "mirroring" in psychology. You are mirroring the person with whom you wish to have rapport. You mimic their speech pattern, their tone of voice, their pace, their mannerism, the way they dress, etc. In reality, we do that all the time. When we wish to speak to a child, we crouch down and speak to the child face to face at the same level. This approach tends to get better results than when we tower over the child and shout out commands.

16. <u>Understand the difference between accuracy and precision</u>. In your presentation, you should use accurate statements with the proper amount of precision necessary to tell your story. The following example illustrates the point. If you are giving direction to someone who is trying to reach the Los Angeles Airport from San Diego, here are three possible directions:

"You can find the Los Angeles Airport in Southern California." This is an accurate statement but it lacks sufficient precision to be of any benefit to the driver.

"You can get to the Los Angeles Airport from San Diego by taking 405 North and going for 125 miles. There will be signs along the freeway to direct you to the airport." This is an accurate statement with proper amount of precision to get the driver to his destination.

"The Los Angeles Airport is located at 33° 56' N and 118° 24' W. in Southern California." This statement is also accurate but probably has too much precision for the driver. It is not necessary to provide the longitude and latitude.

17. <u>Keep your presentation SIMPLE</u>. Keep it simple and good things will happen. This is one of the many sound advices given in the book "The Power of Simplicity" by Jack Trout. Simplicity is at the heart of many success stories in business. Here are some examples of simplicity at work:

One of the reasons for Papa John's Pizza's success is that it keeps its operation simple. Every location has the same mixer, same water purification system, same oven and same computer system. It makes operation that much simpler for everyone involved.

Southwest Airlines has similar simplicity at work. By flying the same model aircraft in its fleet, it makes maintenance and training much easier. It keeps its spare parts inventory down. The airline has no assigned seating. That makes boarding the plane quicker and it shortens the turnaround time at the gate. That in turn translates to higher utilization rate for its airplanes and greater profit.

Simplicity is key in both examples.

Always present your ideas in bite size chunks. Never lump ideas together . Here is an example:

Will your audience understand you when you present the following to them?

KGBIBMNASACIAFBIAIGEPA

Probably not. It is too large a chunk to digest. Now if you break this into bite size chunks, you audience will understand it:

KGB IBM NASA CIA FBI AIG EPA

Another elegant example of simplicity is something you see everyday on the Internet. Look at Google's search engine web page and you will see simplicity. There is no clutter. No banner ads. Just type in the term you want to look for in Google.

It is that simple.

Here is what Jack Welch said about simplicity when he was interviewed by the Harvard Business Review in 1989 while he was CEO of General Electric: "*Insecure managers create complexity. Frightened, nervous managers use thick convoluted planning books and busy slides filled with everything they've known since childhood....... They worry that if they're simple, people will think they're simple minded. In reality, of course, it's just the reverse. Clear, tough minded people are the most simple.*"

18. <u>Use common sense in your presentation</u>. Common sense is defined as "native good judgment free from emotional bias or intellectual subtlety." When you are not sure what material to use in your presentation, try to see things as they really are. Don't be too cute or too clever. Use your common sense. If you have that uneasy feeling about including certain material in your presentation, take that as an advice from a friend and don't use it.

19. <u>Limit your corporate overview</u>. Unless your clients specifically ask for it, do not include more than one slide on overview of your company. Many of your future clients are not interested in how many vice presidents you have in your corporate office. They are probably not interested in the history of your firm or your company's mission statement. They are much more interested in how you are going to solve their problems. If they invite you to make a presentation to them, they already know something about your company. What they don't know is your approach to solving their problems. The only time you should show them how many offices you have throughout the world is when you are bidding on a job that requires global reaches.

20. <u>Use Plenty of Examples</u>. Always give examples and be as specific as you can. Instead of telling your audience

what you are saying, SHOW them by way of examples. The fast-food chain Jack in the box has a sustainability page on its website. Most environmental sustainability statements are like mission statements – fuzzy, ill-defined with a bunch of happy talk.

Jack in the box is an exception.

It gives specific examples. It tells the world it has installed smart irrigation controls and low flow kitchen and plumbing fixtures which "could reduce water usage by up to a million gallons a year". It has increased the amount of recycled materials by "more than 20 percent". It has "diverted more than 50 percent" of its corporate office's trash away "from local landfills". It has "decreased electricity usage by more than 7 percent in natural gas usage by 95 percent" at its corporate office. The list goes on. The specific examples with numbers give the audience something to relate to. They can relate to the magnitude of the accomplishment.

Chapter 4: Handling nervousness during the presentation

First of all, don't ever let them see you sweat and never start a presentation with an apology .

The best antidote to nervousness is a combination of knowledge and preparation. If you know the topics being presented, you will be able to speak about it with confidence. If you have done your homework and have thought about the questions that might be asked of you at the presentation, you will be less nervous.

Consider this example: What would happen to you if someone handed you some detailed notes on Einstein's Theory of Relativity and ask you to make a presentation to a group of physicists and be prepared to answer any questions on the topic? It would be very natural for you to have extreme anxiety unless you are a physicist and you are thoroughly familiar with the Theory of Relativity. You can stay up all night and memorize the entire theory and the next morning you may be able to give a flawless

presentation. But what if someone in the audience asks you a question, will you have the knowledge to answer it?

Memorizing your speech will not help you. In fact, it will make you more nervous. While you are reciting your memorized speech, you will be dreading the moment when someone asks you a question you know you cannot answer.

The moral of this story is that you have to have knowledge of the topic you are presenting.

It is very common to have stage fright. Even accomplished public speakers feel that anxiety pang before getting on the podium. They have butterflies in their stomachs and sweaty hands – just like everybody else.

The nervousness comes from a fear of the unknown – of not knowing how a group of total strangers will react to their presentation. It is a very natural and normal response. All speakers have it. What sets the good speakers apart from the bad ones is that they are able to manage or minimize that fear.

Here are some practical ideas on how to do just that:

1. A very effective way to overcome your nervousness is to think about the last time you accomplished something with great confidence. Relive that moment in your mind. Play it back in your head when you are on stage. Some people have found that if they "anchor" that feeling of confidence to some tangible action like tucking at their sleeves or holding onto a pointer, they can relive that same confident moment during their presentation. Use whatever anchor that works for you.

2. Another very effective way to overcome stage fright is to get to know your audience <u>before</u> you speak. If you are making a sales presentation before a company, try to learn as much as possible about your clients and their organization. At a minimum, get background information about the company. Find out what products it makes or service it provides. It is exactly like going to a job

interview. You want to impress your future employer with your knowledge of his company. If you know the names of the people on the selection panel, Google them and find out more about them. The point here is to make yourself feel as comfortable as possible about the people to whom you are going to be presenting. It makes your future clients a little bit less like complete "total strangers" to you. This is the reason many successful public speakers make a point of mingling with the audience before getting up on the podium. It is a great way to overcome the fear of the "unknown".

3. Try to focus on the presentation and not on yourself. Your presentation is not all about you. Remember that your future clients are judging your presentation based on your knowledge and ability to answer their questions. They are not there to rate you as an orator. If you know the topic, you will not be nervous. If you are not familiar with the topic of your presentation, no amount of rehearsal will save you. That's why doing your homework is the key. Knowledge brings confidence and confidence overcomes nervousness.

4. Establish and maintain eye contact with your audience. Speak to them as if they are your colleagues or friends. The more "contacts" – both verbal and non-verbal - you have with your audience, the less they seem like "total strangers" to you. Always treat your presentation as a conversation with your audience. Pick out one or two persons in the audience at a time and make good eye contacts with them and do your presentation as if you are talking to them.

5. Remember that stage fright is most pronounced before you speak. It is a feeling generated by uncertainty. People who are not able to overcome their stage fright often believe erroneously that the fear they have before

they speak will get worse once they get on the podium. The reverse is true. The butterflies in your stomach will fly away and your sweaty hands will dry up once you get into talking about topics that you know so well. Also remember that very often your audience will not even notice how nervous you are. We are often a much harsher critic of our own performance. That's why you should never tell your audience that you are nervous or apologize. Why tell them you are nervous if they don't even know you are nervous.

6. If your lead technical person on the presentation team is too nervous to lead the presentation, you can use one of your most confident and knowledgeable team members as a "Master of Ceremonies" (MC). This person can lead off the presentation and get things rolling, which will settle the nerves of other presenters. The MC can also direct questions and interject, when needed.

About the Author

Norman Wei is an environmental consultant who makes his living giving 2-day long seminars on highly technical subjects. He uses slide presentations in his classes with Keynotes on his MacBook and iPad. There are no bullet points in any of his slide presentations and his audience loves it.

The material in this booklet is taken from his new book "Selling to Your Clients" due out in January 2012.

His book is written from the perspective of someone who has hired and fired numerous consultants and contractors as a corporate manager. It details all the dos and donts in the consultants' quest for new clients. It includes 13 most common fatal mistakes made by consultants.

Norman is available for onsite seminars on the following topics:

I. How to make connection with your future clients
II. How to make effective PowerPoint presentations
III. The 13 most common mistakes made by consultants
IV. How to select your consultants

He can be reached at 360-490-6828 or by email at norman@normanwei.com

His website is http://www.normanwei.com. He writes a blog on "Excellence in Presentation". He is based in Cape Coral, Florida.

www.ingramcontent.com/pod-product-compliance
Lightning Source LLC
Chambersburg PA
CBHW020948180526
45163CB00006B/2366